Learning to Write
Persuasive Paragraphs

Frances Purslow

Weigl

CALGARY
www.weigl.com

Published by Weigl Educational Publishers Limited
6325 10 Street SE
Calgary, Alberta, Canada T2H 2Z9

Website: www.weigl.com

Library and Archives Canada Cataloguing in Publication Data

Purslow, Frances
    Persuasive paragraphs / Frances Purslow.

ISBN 978-1-55388-438-5 (bound).--ISBN 978-1-55388-439-2 (pbk.)

    1. Persuasion (Rhetoric)--Juvenile literature. 2. English
language--Paragraphs--Juvenile literature. 3. Composition (Language
arts)--Juvenile literature. I. Title.
PE1439.P874 2008   j808'.042   C2008-901429-4

Printed in the United States of America
1 2 3 4 5 6 7 8 9 0 12 11 10 09 08

Editor: Heather Kissock
Design: Terry Paulhus

Photograph Credits
Every reasonable effort has been made to trace ownership and to obtain permission to reprint copyright material.
The publishers would be pleased to have any errors or omissions brought to their attention so that they may be
corrected in subsequent printings.

Alamy: page 9; **Getty Images:** pages 3, 4, 5, 6, 7, 8, 10, 11, 12, 13, 15, 16, 17, 18, 20, 21; **Library and Archives
Canada:** pages 14 (C-085854), 19 (C-000803).

We acknowledge the financial support of the Government of Canada through the Book Publishing Industry
Development Program (BPIDP) for our publishing activities.

Table of Contents

What is a Persuasive Paragraph?

A persuasive paragraph is a group of sentences used to convince someone to believe or do something. It begins with a statement that is an **opinion** or belief. Then, it offers facts to support this belief or opinion. The purpose of a persuasive paragraph is to sway the reader to agree with the author. This type of paragraph may be complete by itself, or it may be part of a longer piece of writing, such as a story.

The following is an example of a persuasive paragraph about the gold rush in the Yukon.

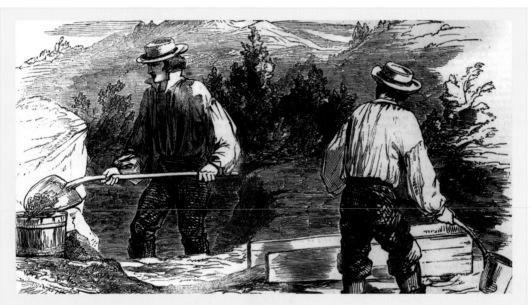

The local miners were the luckiest. They were the first to arrive at the gold sites. At a time when people were making about 10 cents an hour, an ounce of gold was worth about $16. In the early months of the gold rush, miners could make one month's salary by finding one nugget of gold. Many of the miners who arrived at a later date went home with nothing because most of the easy gold was gone. They were not lucky.

What is the writer trying to convince the readers to think? Find the facts that prove the miners who lived closest to the gold fields made the most money.

Stating an Opinion or Belief

The following persuasive paragraph is about the life of gold miners. By saying the miners had a hard life, the writer is expressing an opinion. The writer supports this belief with sentences that state the facts.

The miners had a hard life. Camps were often crowded and full of diseases. Supplies and food were expensive. The men did not have enough to eat. Every day, they worked long hours panning for gold. It was challenging work that was not fun. The miners were often exhausted. They had to carry heavy packs.

What can you tell from the image of miners travelling to a new dig site during the Yukon Gold Rush? Look for clues that support your belief. Make a list of your beliefs and supporting facts.

What Are Nouns?

A persuasive paragraph is usually about a person, place, or thing. The paragraphs about the gold rush are about the event, miners, sites, fortune, and the Yukon. Each of these words refers to a person, place, or thing. These words are called nouns.

Read the following persuasive paragraph about early **homesteaders**. In 1872, the Canadian government drew up the Dominion Lands Act. According to the act, each homesteader could claim 65 hectares of land for $10. This attracted people from all over the world.

In the example, the red words are nouns. They refer to something or someone. Look at the photo of the early homesteaders. List some of the nouns you see there.

Early settlers felt quite alone. Homesteads were often miles apart. Some people felt it was too far to walk. Still, neighbours made an effort to see each other. Neighbours shared farm work. They helped each other build homes and gather crops. They ran errands for each other.

Learning about Proper Nouns

Read the following paragraph about Canada's early settlers. Notice the words that begin with capital letters.

In the late 1400s, explorers from Europe came to North America. Their explorations revealed that it was a land rich in natural resources, including fish and furs. Over time, European explorers, fishers, and fur traders claimed lands in North America for France and Great Britain. The British built early fishing settlements in what is now Newfoundland and Labrador, and in parts of the present-day United States. The French built settlements in present-day Nova Scotia, Prince Edward Island, and New Brunswick. They called this area Acadia. The French also built settlements along the St. Lawrence River and around the Great Lakes. This area was known as New France.

"Europe," "North America," "France," "Great Britain," "British," "European," "Newfoundland," "Labrador," "United States," "French," "Nova Scotia," "Prince Edward Island," "New Brunswick," "Acadia," "St. Lawrence River," "Great Lakes," and "New France" begin with capital letters even though they are found in the middle or at the end of the sentences. These are the names of specific people, places, or things. They are called proper nouns. Proper nouns always begin with a capital letter.

Visit **www.collectionscanada.ca/settlement/kids**, and research other sites to learn more about Canada's early settlers. Where did other settlers come from? The names of their countries are proper nouns.

Fact Versus Opinion

Every day, people see, read, or hear messages. Advertisements on television try to convince people to buy certain products. It is important to judge whether the message is a fact or an opinion. Persuasive messages use facts, opinions, or a combination of both to **influence** people.

Facts are statements that can be proven. They are true statements about things that actually exist or events that have really happened. Opinions are statements of belief. Opinions may or may not be supported by facts.

The following paragraph tells about settlers' journeys across Canada.

Settlers felt a sense of pride when they completed the journey to their new homestead. Often, they were discouraged by the challenges on the trail. The journey could take four to six months and involved many hardships. Settlers travelled in groups called wagon trains. As many as 250 people travelled in one wagon train. Each group chose one guide and one captain to lead the wagon train.

The first sentence is an opinion because some people might have felt differently about finishing the journey. The last sentence is a fact because it can be proven. Now, review the other sentences in the paragraph. Are they fact or opinion?

Using Fact and Opinion to Make a Statement

Read the following persuasive paragraph about Acadia, which was a major settlement in early Canada. Decide which statements are opinions and which are facts. Remember to think about which of the statements can be proven.

*France and England competed with each other to control Acadia. Often, wars in Europe decided who controlled the area. In 1713, a peace **treaty** divided Acadia between the English and the French. The English gained control of the area now known as Nova Scotia. They demanded an oath of **loyalty** from the Acadian settlers who lived there. The Acadians refused to swear this oath. They believed the English would make them fight against the French if a war occurred. Instead, the Acadians agreed to stay **neutral** in times of war. The English accepted this at first, but they were afraid the Acadians would help the French if war did occur. In 1755, the English forced all Acadians to leave Nova Scotia. The Acadians were upset. They had not been treated fairly.*

Parts of a Persuasive Paragraph

A persuasive paragraph has three parts. The first part is the topic sentence. The topic sentence is usually the first sentence. It states an opinion. The topic sentence tells readers what the writer would like them to think or do.

Supporting sentences generally follow the topic sentence. They provide reasons to convince readers that the opinion is correct. The reasons should be supported by facts, examples, or information from experts.

At the end of a persuasive paragraph, a sentence wraps up, or summarizes, the ideas expressed in the paragraph. This is called the concluding sentence. It is usually a strong statement. Sometimes, the writer uses the concluding sentence to state what he or she wants the readers to do if they accept his or her ideas.

The topic sentence is shown in red in the paragraph about women on homesteads. Can you tell which are the supporting and concluding sentences?

*Women worked just as hard as men on homesteads. They ran the households and cared for the children. They cooked meals, milked cows, and washed clothes. In their gardens, they grew vegetables, which they **preserved** for winter. Women also made candles for lighting their homes and soap for washing. Women of the early West had little time to rest. They often felt there was not enough time to complete their chores.*

Identifying the Parts

Look at the photo, and write a topic sentence about early settlers. Then, write two or three supporting sentences to convince readers that the opinion is correct. Finally, write a strong concluding sentence.

Types of Sentences

Using different sentence types adds variety and interest to persuasive paragraphs. There are four basic kinds of sentences. They are telling sentences, asking sentences, commanding sentences, and exclaiming sentences.

A telling sentence provides information. It makes a statement. A telling sentence ends with a period.

An asking sentence asks a question. It ends with a question mark.

A commanding sentence gives a command or makes a request. It ends with a period, unless it is a forceful command. A forceful command ends with an exclamation mark.

An exclaiming sentence shows fear, surprise, excitement, or another strong feeling. It also ends with an exclamation mark.

Can you identify the types of sentences used in the box below?

To receive land, homesteaders had to follow the rules set out by the government.

In what kind of homes did homesteaders live while travelling in wagon trains?

Please start a fire to cook dinner.

The flames are too hot!

Using Proper Ending Punctuation

Read the following sentences. What is the correct ending punctuation?

1. Homesteaders worked hard to develop their farms
2. I have never seen so many grasshoppers
3. Why would weather be important to homesteaders
4. Do not go out in that blizzard without a coat
5. Settler children played hide-and-seek when their chores were done
6. Look at those tiny sod houses
7. Who was the first person to claim a homestead
8. Please bring in some wood for the stove

Now, look at the picture. Write a telling, asking, commanding, and exclaiming sentence based on what you see. Be sure to use the proper ending punctuation.

Understanding Unity

All of the sentences in a persuasive paragraph should relate to the same topic. This is called unity. If a paragraph does not have unity, then one or more sentences do not relate to the main idea. The following persuasive paragraph has unity. All of the sentences explain how the Canadian government was able to attract people to come to Canada to settle the land.

*Clifford Sifton, Canada's minister in charge of **immigration** in the late 1800s, had a brilliant plan to attract settlers to Canada. Sifton launched a huge advertising campaign to attract settlers from Britain, the American West, and Europe. He offered extra money to steamship companies for every immigrant they carried. The results were staggering. About 2 million people from around the world moved to Canada, and most of them settled in the West. Sifton's plan was an astounding success.*

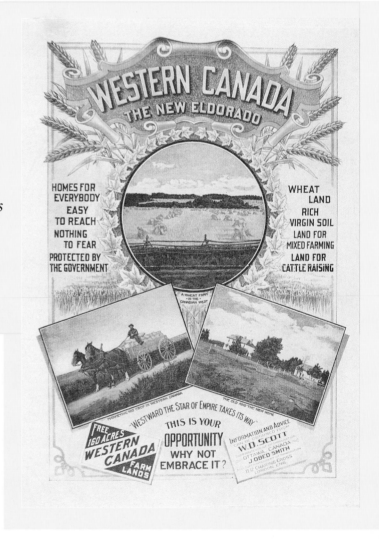

Look at the poster used to attract settlers to Canada in the late 1800s. What words does it use to persuade the reader?

Which Sentence Does Not Belong?

The following paragraph does not have unity. It includes a sentence that does not relate to the main topic. Find the sentence that is out of place in this persuasive paragraph.

The boat trip across the ocean was a frightening experience. The voyage from Scotland to Canada took many weeks. Edinburgh is the capital city of Scotland. There was no land to be seen in all that time. Also, the seas were often rough, especially if the crossing was made in winter. How high the waves were! They sometimes made the boat seem very small. Immigrants had to be brave to take on such a voyage. They left their old life behind and did not know what to expect when they landed.

The website **www.pier21.ca** has many facts about the immigrants who travelled by ship to Halifax. Use information from this website to write a persuasive paragraph convincing others to come to Canada or to remain in their home countries. Make sure that the paragraph has unity.

Creating Coherence

The ideas in a paragraph should flow in a logical order from beginning to end. This is called coherence. Connecting words, such as "then," "next," and "finally," help show the order of time. These connecting words are called transitions. They connect the sentences and show the sequence of events.

Other transitions can be used to describe something in order of place, such as "nearby," "above," "inside," and "at the top."

The following persuasive paragraph has coherence. It tells about Oktoberfest. The paragraph flows in a logical order of time. Notice the transitions that show the order of time.

*Oktoberfest is a popular festival in Germany. Many German people immigrated to Canada during the 1700s, 1800s, and 1900s. They brought many of their **traditions**, including Oktoberfest. In October of every year, Canadians of German descent hold Oktoberfest celebrations to give thanks for successful harvests and to honour their German **heritage**. Parades, dances, and music are a big part of the celebrations. Many people have fun at Oktoberfest. Today, Oktoberfest celebrations are held across the country.*

Put These Sentences in Order

The following sentences describe a family tradition. Can you figure out the correct order of the sentences to create a persuasive paragraph with coherence? Look for clues to the correct order.

A. A family recipe is a thing to be treasured. When my great-grandmother left Poland many years ago, she brought with her a recipe for potato pancakes. It was not written down. It was only in Great-grandmother's memory.

B. Now, my mother is going to teach me how to make this family recipe.

C. When my grandmother married, Great-grandmother taught her how to make these special pancakes.

D. Then, my grandmother passed the recipe on to her daughter, my mother.

E. I am very lucky to be part of this tradition.

Tools for Paragraph Writing

What did you learn? Look at the questions in the "Skills" column. Compare them to the page number in the "Page" column. Refresh your memory about the content you learned during this part of the paragraph writing process by reading the "Content" column below.

SKILLS	CONTENT	PAGE
What is a persuasive paragraph?	gold miners	4–5
What are nouns?	Dominion Lands Act, European settlement	6–7
What is a fact? What is an opinion?	wagon trains, Acadians	8–9
What are the parts of a persuasive paragraph?	the life of women settlers	10–11
What are the four types of sentences?	homesteaders	12–13
What is unity?	immigration	14–15
What is coherence?	Oktoberfest, potato pancakes	16–17

Practise Writing Different Types of Sentences

Look at the drawing of the Aboriginal settlement and the ships in the distance. Write four sentences based on the image. Two of the sentences should include an opinion. The other two should include facts. The four sentences should be a telling sentence, an asking sentence, an exclaiming sentence, and a commanding sentence.

*The Acadians would not have survived if not for the Mi'kmaq **Aboriginal Peoples**. The Mi'kmaq taught Acadians how to use canoes, toboggans, and snowshoes. They also acted as guides when Acadians needed to explore or travel. The Mi'kmaq showed the settlers how to hunt and where to fish. They showed the Acadians which plants were safe to eat and which could be used to make medicine. The Acadians were grateful to the Mi'kmaq for their help in their new home.*

Put Your Knowledge to Use

Put your knowledge of persuasive paragraphs to use by writing a paragraph about what you think life might have been like for a settler or early immigrant.

Here is a photograph of an early cowboy. The paragraph about cowboys and ranching has a topic sentence, supporting sentences, and a concluding sentence. The sentences flow in a logical order and are related to each other. There are many nouns throughout the text.

*Life on a ranch was exciting. Ranchers raised **livestock** to help feed the townspeople. They also tamed horses. Cities and towns began to grow quickly in the late 1800s. The ranching industry grew. Thousands of cowboys were hired to work on ranches. Cowboys enjoyed working on ranches. They fixed fences and cleaned stables. It was hard work, but cowboys thought it was worth the effort.*

Select one of the photos, and write a persuasive paragraph. List the reasons and facts that support the statement you want people to believe. As you write your paragraph, make sure that it has a topic sentence, supporting sentences, and a concluding sentence. Choose only sentences that relate to your topic, and be sure that the ideas in your paragraph flow in a logical order from beginning to end. Add variety and interest by including various types of sentences.

EXPANDED CHECKLIST

Reread your paragraph, and make sure that you have all of the following.

- ☑ My paragraph has a topic sentence.
- ☑ My paragraph has supporting sentences.
- ☑ My paragraph has a concluding sentence.
- ☑ All of the sentences in my paragraph relate to the same topic.
- ☑ All of the ideas in my paragraph flow in a logical order.
- ☑ My paragraph has sentence variety.

Types of Paragraphs

Now you have learned the tools for writing persuasive paragraphs. You can use your knowledge of nouns, facts and opinions, parts of a paragraph, unity, and coherence to write persuasive paragraphs. There are three other types of paragraphs. You can use some of the same tools you learned in this book to write all types of paragraphs. The chart below shows other types of paragraphs and their key features.

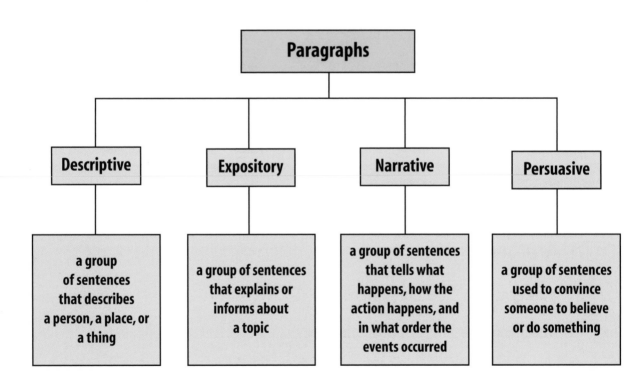

Paragraphs

Descriptive

a group of sentences that describes a person, a place, or a thing

Expository

a group of sentences that explains or informs about a topic

Narrative

a group of sentences that tells what happens, how the action happens, and in what order the events occurred

Persuasive

a group of sentences used to convince someone to believe or do something

Websites for Further Research

Many books and websites provide information on writing persuasive paragraphs. To learn more about writing this type of paragraph, borrow books from the library, or surf the Internet.

To find out more about writing persuasive paragraphs, type key words, such as "writing paragraphs" into the search field of your Web browser. There are many sites that teach about early Canadian settlers and immigrants. You can use these sites to practise writing persuasive paragraphs. Begin by selecting one topic from the site. Read about the topic, and then use the checklist on page 21 to write a paragraph.

Visit *The Canadian Encyclopedia* to learn more about early Canadian immigrants.
www.thecanadianencyclopedia.com

Canada: A People's History Online provides first-hand accounts, images, and information about early Canadian settlers.
http://history.cbc.ca

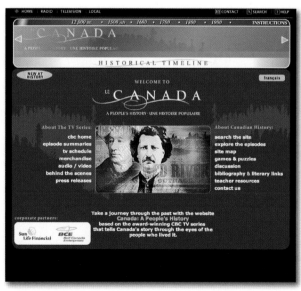

Glossary

Aboriginal Peoples: original inhabitants of a country

heritage: something handed down to people from their ancestors

homesteaders: people who settled on land given to settlers

immigration: coming into a country to live

influence: to produce an effect on the behaviour of others

livestock: farm animals raised for sale

loyalty: faithfulness

neutral: not taking sides

opinion: a view or judgment that is formed about someone or something and is not necessarily based on fact

preserved: prepared for long-term storage or kept in its original form

traditions: customs passed down from parents to children

treaty: an agreement between countries

Index